A Comprehensive Guide

CW00742949

Conten

Contents

Contents

Acknowledgements

My grateful thanks go to Ivor Hughes, Julie Morland, Charles Salkield, Audrey Felton, Paula Parke, Linda Aston and Diana Brown for their assistance and advice during the writing and publishing of this book.

First published in Great Britain in 1996 by :

Hughes Publishing Group
West Molesey, Surrey KT8 1PD.

Introduction.

Guinea-pigs, or Cavies as they are sometimes known, are one of the most underrated pets I know. Often overlooked in favour of other small animals, people do not realise what super companions they can be if looked after correctly.

Although generally kept outdoors guinea-pigs do in fact make ideal indoor pets as they are clean and odourless. They are also one of the more modestly priced pets available. You will of course need to purchase housing, accessories and food but the costs of these are comparable with those of purchasing any small animal. The advantage of a guinea-pig is that they are comparatively long-lived and so you will have a friend and companion for several years and not just a couple.

With their extensive vocabulary of grunts, squeals and purrs and expressive body language guinea-pigs are among the most entertaining and intelligent pets. An observant owner will soon recognise what it is their pet is saying and derive enormous pleasure from watching and learning from him.

Guinea-pigs can be very affectionate and do not jump and seldom bite. They come in a variety of colours and textures so there is a breed to suit each individual taste. The Rexes make wonderful children's pets, with their cute teddy bear faces and wiry hair.

Susie, a Buff Satin Guinea-Pig.

A dark eyed white, a pink eyed white
and a cinnamon Agouti (not purebred).

The Peruvian comes with long silky locks which grows forward over the face producing a comical "Dougal" character whereas in the Sheltie, its long hair sweeps back over its body. The marked short-haired breeds such as Tortoiseshell, Dutch and Himalayan, have colours in a precise pattern, perfect for owners who want an attractive pet which requires less grooming.

For those people who like to have something different, there are the newer breeds with wonderful names which match their appearance, like Texels, Merinos, Satins, and Alpacas.

I hope that by the end of this book the reader will have a greater appreciation and understanding of these endearing little animals. For ease of reading I have referred to guinea-pigs in the singular or as "him".

Two supremely healthy pet Guinea-Pigs.
Note the well rounded body of "Pebbles" (above)
and the glossy coat of "Liquorice" (below).

4

Purchasing

Ideally your guinea-pig should be purchased when it is between 6-8 weeks old. Always consider buying more than one, provided you have the available room because guinea-pigs are gregarious creatures who enjoy company.

Don't buy on the spur of the moment without thinking about the long-term commitment to your pet. With good care guinea-pigs should live for at least 4 or 5 years.

Pet or Pure-Bred?

It is equally important that you are completely happy with your choice. Look at all the varieties available and think about whether you would prefer to buy from a reputable breeder or a good Pet Shop. A good Pet Shop is one in which all sale stock is kept in clean cages with plenty of dried and fresh food to eat and a clean bottle full of water. The boars and sows should be displayed in separate cages and not in with rabbits. A conscientious Proprietor would ensure that literature on how to care for new pets is also readily available.

Pet shops usually stock guinea-pigs which do not quite match up to the breed standard for that particular variety but, nevertheless, make excellent pets. However the pet shop may only keep stock from a few breeding sources and will not be in a position to offer a wide choice of varieties.

Guinea-Pig companions

If you wish to purchase a purebred pet or a rarer variety, then find out whether there are any local Cavy Shows, (sometimes combined rabbit and cavy shows). Go along and see the breeds available and talk to the breeders. There are shows of this nature all year round and they are advertised in specialist Pet magazines. By observing the animals exhibited at a show you can be assured that your final choice is the right one.

Choosing Your Guinea-Pig

When choosing your pet, observe his behaviour in the cage. Whether he is in a cage on his own or in with companions he will probably rush away as you approach. This is normal. Guinea-pigs are naturally shy animals and so this caution means that your guinea-pig is alert and has a good sense of hearing. Check the way the guinea-pig moves, he should not limp or hop, but run swiftly.

Pick your guinea-pig up and examine him carefully. His eyes should be clear and bright with no discharge. The eyeball should not appear opaque or have a white centre as this is indicative of cataracts. The ears should be clean inside with no build up of wax. The nose should be dry and clean.

Check his mouth. It should not hang open and there should be no sign of sores. Any staining around an otherwise healthy mouth is probably from the food he has eaten such as carrot or beetroot and is nothing to worry about. The teeth are also important. They should be of an even length, not misshapen or broken.

Look carefully at his coat and skin. Run your finger through his hair from back to front. It will feel clean and look shiny on a healthy animal. The skin will be light pink on a light haired guinea-pig and dark on a dark haired pig. There should be no bald patches, greasy looking hair, dry flaky skin or excessive pinkness of skin. These are signs of skin disease and to be avoided.

Your guinea-pig should feel solid with his bones well padded with flesh. His anus should be clean with no sign of diarrhoea. His feet should not be caked in filth or be red and blistered looking.

Boars or Sows?

Boars are best kept singly or in pairs because when they mature they are more inclined to battle for dominance. If housing space is limited or cost of upkeep an important factor, then purchasing one or two boars will be a good idea as their inquisitive and outgoing personalities means they make wonderfully tame pets if handled regularly.

Sows enjoy the company of other sows and can be kept in pairs, trios or any manageable number in a suitably sized cage. Sometimes you may have one sow who will not tolerate the presence of any other pig. She may behave very aggressively to other guinea-pigs but will be wonderfully docile with humans. If this is the case she will have to be housed separately.

Sexing

Sexing guinea-pigs is relatively easy, even from quite a young age. A sow's genital area is an oval area of soft almost hairless skin with a Y-shaped opening. The boar's genital area is similar but the opening in the boar is like an upside down exclamation mark (!) with the dot being the penis and the vertical slit the anal opening. The penis can be extruded on quite young boars with gentle pressure just in front of the genital area. In older boars the testes become more obvious on each side of the anal opening. Both boars and sows have one pair of nipples (pictures page 10).

Companions

Contrary to popular belief rabbits and guinea-pigs do not make good companions. The injuries rabbits cause to guinea-pigs kicking out with their hind legs and overzealous grooming, resulting in nasty bites along the back of the neck, will make your pig a nervous wreck. Cracked ribs, internal injuries and possibly death may result.

Some rabbits continuously pester guinea-pigs to try to mate with them which does not provide a happy existence either. The best companion for a guinea-pig is another guinea-pig!

Introducing New Friends

You can introduce a new young guinea-pig to an older one but take a few precautions and make sure you keep an eye on them to ensure that there are no problems.

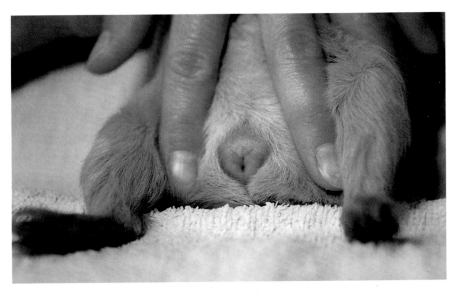

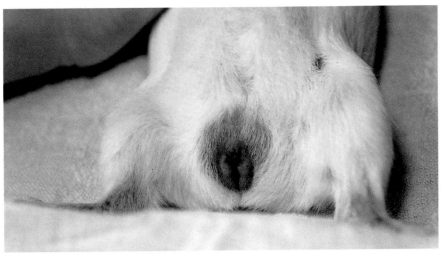

Sexing Guinea-Pigs
Top picture shows a Sow indicating the Y shape
Below is a Boar.

Washing the new animal in a mild shampoo suitable for pets will mask his natural smell and so lessen the chance of aggression. Try to introduce them on neutral territory, a grass run is a good idea, or at least in a newly cleaned cage with lots of fresh and dry food. This will divert their attention from one another.

Behaviour

Watching a large group of guinea-pigs interact with one another is a fascinating and amusing pastime. I have watched a group of about six sows all squabbling over a small cardboard box that I placed in their enclosure. They all wanted to sit in it but there was simply not enough room. They all crammed themselves inside, some on top of others all in the most uncomfortable positions. Not one was willing to budge so in the end I had to remove the box altogether to prevent further argument.

On another occasion I placed a long tube in the run for them to play in. One sow parked herself at the entrance and another at the exit and neither would allow any other pig inside the tube, but guarded their end resolutely.

Several other pigs milled around in the background waiting for an opportunity to overthrow the guards. At last one guard sows attention was diverted by another pig who, tired of waiting had given her a head butt on the rump. She turned to her attacker and as she did so one of the smaller pigs rushed into the tube. Pandemonium reigned!

Vocabulary

One of the most enchanting aspects of keeping guinea-pigs is the amazing range of vocal noises they make. Many small pets are comparatively silent and so a guinea-pig's habit of welcoming your approach to his cage with a high volume volley of squeaks is very endearing.

You will soon learn that the high pitched repetitive "weet-weet" noise means "Here I am, have you got a tasty titbit for me?" A low chuckle signifies pleasure, usually over a favourite food.

Sows also make this noise when they are suckling their litter. A short, loud "brurr" noise is an alarm signal. All the other guinea-pigs are immediately on the alert. Perhaps a cat has passed too close or they have been startled by a loud noise. It can also be a sign of displeasure for example, if you insist on brushing your pets coat the wrong way.

Young ones when reprimanded by a nip from an adult, make a mewing sound, eyes closed, head twisted, shuffling from one foot to the other as if in mortal agony. This lasts maybe a few seconds then suddenly, as if coming out of a trance they trot off quite happily! Two boars in confrontation will gnash their teeth at one another in a chattering warning. A boar, when trying to mate a sow will make a low vibrating purr weaving his body around the sow.

One very unusual noise you may hear from your guinea-pig, and one that appears to be confined to sows is a strange "chirping" like a bird. It is very loud and alarms both the guinea-pig who is making the noise and its companions.

I have no idea why some guinea-pigs make this noise or what triggers it, indeed I have only heard it once in my experience of keeping around 40 pigs. The guinea-pig is not ill and once it has stopped chirping it continues to behave normally.

There is much to learn from guinea-pigs and that is half the fun of keeping them. Their public image of being dull and boring could not be more wrong.

Housing

Situation

Please don't confine your pet to a hutch at the bottom of the garden. It will only result in its care becoming a chore instead of a pleasure.

The ideal solution is to house your pet indoors, as mentioned earlier. You can purchase indoor cages with plastic trays and wire sides and tops, similar but larger than hamster cages. These cages will house 1 to 3 adult guinea-pigs. Otherwise an untreated plywood hutch can be used. You should always buy the largest cage you can afford. Other advantages of housing guinea-pigs indoors are that any health problems will be noticed right away as will any skirmishes between groups of pigs.

If you house your pet outdoors, situate the hutch as close to the back door as possible, but bear in mind that the hutch should not face due south or be in a very exposed windy position. A shed or outhouse could be ideal provided it is adequately ventilated and not too dark or too hot in summer. It will provide shelter for your pet during winter months. Garages may be suitable so long as they are not used for parking cars and have adequate light and ventilation.

Whichever accommodation you choose, your pet must be kept warm and dry. Damp is very dangerous to guinea-pigs leading to respiratory and skin disease.

A Sturdy Outdoor Hutch with felt roof & sleeping area
& a selection of indoor cages suitable for Guinea-Pigs.

Type of Accommodation

The outdoor hutch should be of solid construction with a felt roof and painted with non-toxic weather-proof paint. A pull-down plastic cover to protect the inside of the cage from becoming wet or draughty at night is a good idea. Inside the cage should have a separate sleeping section for extra warmth at night. A litter board is useful to prevent hay falling out of the cage whenever the door is opened. A strip of wood about 3 inches high that can be lifted out for cleaning and slotted back into place afterwards is ideal. Litter boards also help prevent your pet falling or leaping out of the cage.

As guinea-pigs need regular exercise you must either purchase or make a run for the garden or indoors. Chicken wire mesh of 1/2" or 1" diameter is ideal for an outdoor run with a hinged lid for easy access and handles for moving onto fresh grass as often as necessary.

Some outdoor runs have a covered end which offers shelter should the weather deteriorate, otherwise simply tack a piece of thick plastic sheeting over part of the lid of the run and this will suffice. It is always advisable to have a lid on an outdoor run to prevent your pet being killed by a cat, dog or fox.

If your pets hutch is suitable for outdoor use then he could be left outside in the run all summer with the freedom to go in and out as he pleases. Place the hutch on a couple of bricks to avoid the bottom getting damp and mouldy and provide a ramp or step for him to get in and out of his cage otherwise he will suffer the consequences of leaping out and dropping to the ground!

Indoor runs are simple to make out of any durable, non-edible material. A simple tray shape with a base, four sides and castors on the underneath for ease of movement is fine. The sides need not be more than a foot high. If you have dogs or cats around then a lid is essential. Chicken wire tacked to a square frame and hinged to the sides of the run will prevent tragedies. A thick layer of paper on the bottom and a covering of hay and your indoor run is ready.

Feeding.

Feeding is vitally important to ensure a happy healthy pet. There are good nutritionally balanced foods available from pet shops, some specially formulated for guinea-pigs. They need higher protein mixes than other rodents and Vitamin C as, like humans, they cannot make their own. All rodents including guinea-pigs have teeth which grow continuously and so the dry mix must contain suitable grinding matter to keep their teeth worn to the correct length. Good feeds will contain lumps of biscuit for this purpose.

If you do not use a foodstuff with Vitamin C already added you must provide it in the shape of EXTRA fresh fruit or vegetables on a daily basis. I say "extra" because your guinea-pig must have fresh fruit and vegetables as part of his diet whether the feed contains added Vitamin C or not.

Two different outdoor runs providing
protection from sun, wind and rain.

The amount of dry mix to feed is a generous handful per guinea-pig once daily. Greenstuffs can be fed freely but take note of those which should be restricted or avoided.

Acceptable greenstuffs include greens, green cabbage, cauliflower leaves, kale, Brussels sprouts, broccoli, carrots, apple, celery, cucumber, tomato and lettuce. The last two fed in small amounts only as they may cause tummy upsets if fed in quantity. Never feed guinea-pigs vegetables straight from the fridge or frosted greens as these may cause severe gastric upset. Spinach is not recommended for guinea-pigs other than in minute quantities.

Raw beetroot without the leaves, is also enjoyed by some guinea-pigs and is a good source of Vitamin C but be warned, it turns their urine dark red! Banana in its skin is an excellent source of vitamins and minerals and melon, especially the rind is also readily taken. In summer fresh green grass (unsprayed) must be easily a guinea-pigs favourite food, and is of course free! Clover can be fed freely but dandelions only in small amounts as they are a diuretic.

Never give lawn mowings to guinea-pigs. It may be tempting to pick up a pile of fresh clippings but they are potentially harmful. A lawn mower is indiscriminate in what it mows and there may be quantities of poisonous plants leaves mixed in with the grass. Also lawn clippings break down and decompose very quickly. Think how hot the centre of a pile of mown grass is. Fermenting grass clippings will give guinea-pigs severe bloat and colic.

Guinea-Pigs favourite foods, fresh grass & carrots.

Plants to avoid are bindweed, solanum (potato plant), foxglove, hemlock (similar in appearance to cow parsley), white bryony, hellebore, privet, rhubarb leaves, deadly and woody nightshade, buttercup, ragwort, laburnum (the seed pods may be scattered over the grass) as these are all poisonous. Bulbs are also poisonous, so avoid placing the outdoor run on an area where crocuses, daffodils and tulips have been planted.

Guinea-pigs are usually expert at knowing what is good to eat and what is not but if you are concerned about any of the plants in your garden keep outdoor runs away from flower beds. Invest in a book on Wild Flowers to help you identify plants.

Equally detrimental to your guinea-pigs health are slug pellets, weed killers and insecticidal/fungicidal sprays. Please be sensible if using them and do not place anywhere near the run area or start spraying plants whilst your pets are out on the lawn.

Another vitally important item needed to maintain health and fitness in your guinea-pig is fresh, sweet meadow hay. This must be provided in addition to his bedding material. Some breeders tie up a bundle of hay and attach it to the mesh of the cage or provide a small hay rack for this purpose.

Fresh water should always be provided daily. Bottles are preferable to bowls which are easily fouled or tipped over.

Day to Day Care

Cleaning Out

Cages, particularly, if you have more than one guinea-pig, must be cleaned out at least twice a week. Guinea-pigs will quickly become ill if kept in damp and dirty conditions.

Bedding should consist of a thick layer of newspaper covered in hay, piled high in the bed area and replenished regularly. Sawdust should never be used as it irritates the eyes and can cause impaction problems in boars. Wood-Chips are also not really suitable as they too can be dusty, aggravating the eyes or lungs. Recent information available shows that chippings from certain coniferous trees cause liver disease in rodents.

Straw is not advisable to use as bedding material as the sharp lengths can cause eye injuries unless cut into short lengths. Hay is the most highly recommended material but if you must use straw provide hay as well as it is an important part of your pets diet.

To clean out, remove all old bedding material and wet paper. Allow to air if possible then replace with clean newspaper and a generous covering of hay, piled up in the bed section. Wash the food-bowl to keep it clean and hygenic and rinse out and re-fill the water bottle. A bottle-brush can be used to remove any green algae that grows inside the bottle.

A Long Haired Coronet Guinea-pig
These pigs will require extra grooming.

A long haired Sheltie Guinea-pig.

23

Each season, it is a good idea to disinfect the cage with a non-toxic disinfectant. This helps prevent a build-up of dirt and the possibility of infection. There are some excellent products available specially formulated for pet use. Do ensure however that the cage is completely dry before putting the guinea-pig back.

Grooming

Grooming is dependent upon whether you have a short or long-haired pet. Short-haired guinea-pigs are easier to care for and are certainly recommended for a beginner. You can comb them using a pure bristle brush and plastic or metal comb. Once a week is adequate.

For long-haired pigs daily grooming is necessary. Ensure that it becomes a part of your pets daily routine, say just before his evening meal. Put him on a flat surface, not too far off the ground in case he falls, and give him a good combing paying particular attention to his rear end. Finish by brushing through with a pure bristle brush for an added shine.

Long-haired guinea-pigs coats can grow at the rate of 1 inch per month and so a haircut every 4 weeks is advisable, especially around the hindquarters to avoid the coat becoming tangled and filthy.

Leaving the coat too long and dirty may also predispose the guinea-pig to urine infections. This will be discussed in more detail in the chapter on Health.

Both boars and sows have a grease gland situated in the region where a tail would be found. In boars these areas can become quite dirty, and some boars have more active glands than others. A small amount of washing up liquid is effective for removing the grease. Simply rub it in with a finger, leave for a few minutes and rinse with warm water.

Alternatively, use a hand cleanser of the type used by car mechanics. Rub into the spot, leave for a minute or two, rinse and towel dry. If the skin looks red and sore apply a small amount of herbal skin balm. This balm can be obtained from pet shops which stock herbal products for animals.

Shampooing

Shampooing is a relatively easy job that will result in your pet looking and smelling beautiful ! As with grooming, short-haired guinea-pigs will not need bathing as often as long-haired but it is up to you how often you choose to shampoo your pet. Any shampoo suitable for pets can be used, there are several available on the market, some containing added conditioners or herbal extracts.

The best method of shampooing, and one which is least likely to terrify the guinea-pig, is to fill a sink or basin to a depth of about 3 inches with fairly warm water. Lower the pig into the water and make sure every bit of him is wetted.

Drain away the water and apply the shampoo, avoiding the eye area and paying particular attention to the rear end and grease spot.

Rinse thoroughly with clean warm water either using a shower head or jug and then towel dry. You can finish off the drying using a hairdryer, especially useful for long-haired pigs, or keep him indoors until completely dry, overnight if necessary.

A self cream guinea-pig.

A buff guinea-pig.

Guinea-Pig Varieties

O ver the years breeders have bred many types of guinea-pig. This chapter could not provide a detailed description of every breed and colour variety available, that would require a whole book in itself, but I have attempted to give a brief description of most of the varieties currently bred today.

Guinea-pigs are be divided into two classes: Selfs and Non Selfs. There is another class of Rare Variety in which the new breeds are placed until they can get their own breed standard.

Selfs

SELFS are short coated guinea-pigs of only one solid colour. There should be no contrasting hairs anywhere on the coat and the coat itself should be smooth with no evidence of rosettes or twists in the hair growth. Ears should resemble folded rose petals. Selfs come in dark-eyed or pink-eyed forms, some such as the golden and white are available in both dark or pink eyes. Colours are Black, White, Red, Beige, Lilac, Cream, Golden, Chocolate and Saffron. Newer colours have names such as Slate and Buff.

Non-Selfs

Non-Self covers every other guinea-pig that is not a Self and includes the long-haireds, roughs and satins.

Non-Self Short-Haired

TORTOISESHELL (Torty) guinea-pigs are black and red, TORTOISESHELL AND WHITE (Torty and White) have the added white colour. On show specimens these colours should be in slabs of contrasting colours evenly distributed over the body with no blurred edges.

BI-COLOURED and TRI-COLOURED guinea-pigs are those that have two or three separate patches of colour on the bodies but are not Torty or Torty and White, Himalayan or Dutch. All guinea-pig varieties can be found in bi or tri colours. Colour combinations may be buff and agouti, black, buff and white, agouti and white, and so on.

HIMALAYANS have a white body with black or chocolate points The points are the nose (or smut), ears and toes. In a show specimen the coat has to be as pure white as possible and the points as black or deep milk chocolate in contrast.

DUTCH guinea-pigs are a coloured variety with markings in a precise pattern. The nose blaze, smellers (nose, mouth and chin), and toes are white as is the saddle which should continue around the guinea-pigs body in a straight line. The cheeks, rump, belly, hocks and feet (excepting the toes) should be coloured. The ears should be of a solid colour with no flesh tones (pink areas). Dutch varieties include the solid colours Red, Black, Chocolate, Cream, and the Agoutis: Silver, Golden, Cinnamon, Cream and Lemon.

A red dutch guinea-pig.

A torty and white guinea-pig

AGOUTI guinea-pigs have a single base colour on each hair and a "ticked" tip. The ticking is always lighter than the base colour. Examples are Silver, Golden, and Lemon agoutis which have a black hair shaft with a silver, golden or lemon tip. Other agouti types are the Cinnamon and Cream which have a chocolate hair shaft with a silver or cream tip. On a good specimen the ticking should be even throughout the whole body and the ears be without any flesh tones. Eyes should be dark or dark ruby.

DALMATION guinea-pigs have two colours on their body, black and white. The body should be white with black spots and the head black with a white nose blaze. The spots should be distinct and not blurred. Recently Dalmations have been bred in other colours and not just black and white.

ROANS are guinea-pigs with two hair colours evenly distributed over the body to produce a pastel effect. In contrast the head is a solid colour. A Red roan has a red head and a body with red and white hairs evenly mixed to produce a dusky pink. The black roan has a black head and the body has black and white hairs mixed evenly to produce a silvery grey colour. There should be no banding on the body or spots of solid colour.

SATIN guinea-pigs are a new breed which possess a coat with a very high sheen on it, a mutation which causes the individual hairs to reflect light instead of absorbing it. Most show satins have coats of a solid colour e.g. Ivory, Buff, Cream, Gold and Saffron Satins. The satin gene has however been bred into other varieties including the Himalayan, Crested and Abyssinian.

Sybil - Best Pet Competition Winner

A saffron satin - this is a show guinea-pig.

ARGENTE guinea-pigs are dilute forms of the Agouti. They have pink eyes and possess "ticked" hair shafts with a base colour and a contrasting tip. They come in colours such as Golden/Lilac, Golden/Beige and Lilac/White. They are classed as a Rare Variety at the moment.

Non-Self Rough-Haired

These include the Abyssinian, Crested and Rex guinea-pigs.

The ABYSSINIAN is a short coated guinea-pig whose coat grows in distinct rosettes all over the body. On a show specimen the coat should be harsh and there should be a set number of rosettes. Abyssinians come in many colours including Solid colours, Tortoiseshell, Torty and White, Agouti, Brindle and Bi or Tri-Colour.

Brindled abyssinians have coats with two coloured hairs mingled together over the body in even, dark or light shades. These colours are Red and Black. Depending upon which colour has dominance it will be a light or dark brindle.

CRESTED guinea-pigs are short, smooth haired pigs with a single rosette placed on the head between the ears. The rosette should be perfectly circular with the hairs radiating from a pinpoint centre.

"Tuppence" a torty & white Abyssinian.

"Buttons" a rex guinea-pig.

Cresteds come in many colours and can be bred into both long and short-haired varieties. e.g. You can have a crested Himalayan, a crested Sheltie (known as a Coronet), crested Satins and so on. American Crested guinea-pigs have a solid body colour with a contrastingly coloured crest. They are very striking to look at.

REXES are short haired guinea-pigs whose hairs are crinkled and curly including the whiskers. Like the satin the rex gene is a mutation of the hair producing one which is crinkly instead of smooth. Rexes come in all colours including solid, bi and tri-coloured and agouti. They tend to be large pigs with a cute, cuddly appearance and docile nature. Indeed, in the United States they are known as Teddies. A show rex has a very dense, harsh coat with no flatness and a short curly-haired belly. Its head is blunt with large bold eyes and drooping ears.

The rex gene has in recent years been introduced to long haired breeds of guinea-pig and the resulting "rexed" Sheltie, Peruvian and Coronet are known as Texels, Alpacas and Merinos. These will be discussed under Long-haired breeds.

Non-Self Long-Haired.

PERUVIANS are long-haired guinea-pigs, originally bred from abyssinians. They are attractive guinea-pigs with a rosette on each rump and the long hair (the sweep) flowing outwards on each side from a central parting along the spine. The fringe (frontal) is also long and falls over the face.

"Lara" a beautiful Sheltie shown combed out
for exhibiting on her grooming board.

A Peruvians coat may grow as much as one inch per month resulting in an adult guinea-pig with a coat possibly some 20 inches long. In a show specimen this would be kept wrapped to avoid it being chewed or damaged. The guinea-pig is shown with its hair brushed forward over its face and fanned out around its body so that you cannot tell which end is which !

Peruvians are not for the beginner unless you are prepared to do the regular grooming necessary. If one is to be kept as a pet it is necessary to keep the hair trimmed to a manageable length.

SHELTIES are also long-haired guinea-pigs originating from a cross between a self guinea-pig and a peruvian. In this breed the hair is short on the face and grows back along the body fanning out on each side. There should be no centre parting when a Sheltie is being exhibited.

The head should be broad with large bold eyes and drooping rose petal ears, the hair dense and silky (in the United States they are known as Silkies). If the Sheltie is to be kept as a pet the hair should be kept trimmed.

Both Shelties and Peruvians come in a wide range of colours including solid, bi and tri-coloured, agouti and so on.

The TEXEL is a Sheltie with the rex gene making the coat long, soft and beautifully wavy. The belly is dense and curly. Texels are shown with a centre parting and the coat combed out on each side.

As they are a long-haired breed they require more attention and show specimens have their coats wrapped to keep them clean and in perfect condition.

The ALPACA is a long haired rexed Peruvian and the MERINO a long-haired rexed Coronet. They are new introductions to the world of showing guinea-pigs and at present are shown under the Rare Varieties section.

Exhibiting

S howing guinea-pigs is a hobby for the dedicated breeder or owner and shows are held most weekends all over the country. Exhibiting guinea-pigs can be a rewarding and enjoyable pastime and there are many local and national shows on all year round. You can become a Juvenile or Adult exhibitor depending upon your age.

Join a national club and a local pet club, then as your interest and knowledge expands, you may wish to join some of the purebred clubs. Joining a club will ensure that you receive information on forthcoming events and the latest trends and breeds within the Fancy.

By joining a number of clubs and visiting shows, perhaps just as a onlooker at first, rather than an exhibitor, you can learn everything you need to know about breed standards, what makes a good show animal and the equipment you need to show successfully.

You are not restricted to showing only purebred guinea-pigs. Many clubs have classes for pets as well and it is a good starting point for the beginner. Indeed some keen exhibitors only show pets as they believe that winning an award for a pet is the ultimate acknowledgement of good husbandry.

Health

Don't let this chapter put you off owning guinea-pigs! In the main guinea-pigs are hardy, problem-free animals who live out their lives contentedly giving their owner enormous pleasure and satisfaction. However, as with humans there are a number of minor ailments and injuries to which they may be subject.

The obtaining of healthy stock from a reliable source is a good way to avoid problems in the first place.

In the case of owning one or more guinea-pigs it is most important that you find a Veterinary Surgeon who is knowledgeable about them and understands how to treat them.

The Cambridge Cavy Trust

The Cambridge Cavy Trust was established to provide a much needed source of expert help and information on the health and husbandry of guinea-pigs and other small animals which are kept by thousands of people who are ignorant of their needs, often through no fault of their own but because of the lack of accurate literature and expertise.

The Cambridge Cavy Trust is a registered Charity which cares specifically for guinea-pigs and other rodents including rats, mice, hamsters, gerbils and chinchillas.

The Trust has its own training College and offers a Diploma course on Rodentology to both practising and training Vets and anyone else who has a special interest in guinea-pigs or any of the animals mentioned above and wishes to become a member. (Address and details on page 78)

If your Vet is a trained Rodentologist or is in contact with the CCT or is him or herself a breeder of guinea-pigs then you can be assured of expert care should your pet need it.

Guinea-Pigs as Patients

Guinea-pigs are terrible patients. They will rapidly go downhill if they are ill, sitting hunched in their cage, their coat all fluffed up and lustreless, eyes sunken and dull, food left untouched. Trying to administer medicine to such an individual is fraught with difficulty. They may become completely hysterical wriggling and squealing or go limp with fear.

The most successful way to deal with your guinea-pig, whether it is to syringe feed, administer medicine or simply examine teeth or ears, is to firstly wrap him in a towel just like a baby. Then with the head poking out at one end and all four feet tucked within the towel, your patient is snug and secure and therefore less inclined to panic.

Regular Checks and Medication

Give your pet a thorough physical examination at least once a week checking feet, claws, teeth, eyes and ears, skin and anus. Long-haired guinea-pigs do require extra attention over the short haired varieties. Their hair quickly becomes matted and dirty so always groom them regularly and keep their hair trimmed to a manageable length.

If you keep a number of guinea-pigs regular doses of an anti-parasitic drug and a worming medication are recommended as is regular shampooing. Skin parasites can be picked up from newly introduced stock, exhibitions where a number of guinea-pigs are in close proximity, or from hay. Guinea-pigs fed on grass or kept on lawns during summer months where dogs or foxes are regular visitors need worming routinely.

Suitable medicines can be obtained from your vet and are quick and simple to administer every 2-3 months in rotation.

Record Cards

It is a good idea to keep record cards for all your stock even if you have only one or two guinea-pigs. These cards should contain details such as age, date of birth, sex, variety, medication given, physical defects e.g. cataracts, injuries, pregnancies, number of young and so on.

These record cards are an invaluable account of your pet's life.

Guinea-pigs have four front claws & three rear claws.

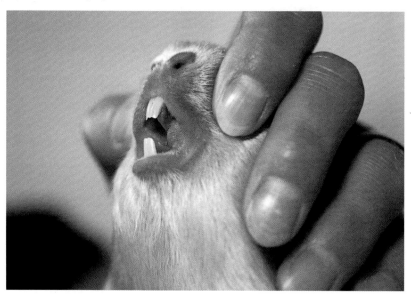

Guinea-pigs have chisel-like front incisors.

43

Feet and Claws

Guinea-pigs have well-padded feet ideal for swift scampering over ground. The front feet have four toes, the back feet three toes although a fourth toe may be present on one or both feet. This is caused by a genetic mutation. These extra digits cause no distress to the guinea-pig unless they become injured or are constantly getting caught.

Claw Clipping

Guinea-pigs claws should become worn down with regular exercise. If they do grow too long and curve inwards they can be easily clipped. It is best to get an expert to do this the first time but thereafter you can do it yourself at home using toenail clippers. Just remember that a blood vessel runs part of the way down the claw. If you cut too close to this vessel there will be considerable bleeding. It is much wiser to cut off less rather than more and to repeat at regular intervals

If you do accidentally cut off too much and the claw bleeds, staunch it under cold running water. Then after drying carefully, dab some vaseline or herbal skin balm (this contains tea tree oil, a natural antiseptic) on the cut end of the claw to seal the blood vessel and help prevent infection.

Sore Soles

The soles of a guinea-pigs feet may become red and blistered looking. There are many possible causes. If your pet is kept in a damp, dirty cage the ammonia in the urine will cause the skin to become red and inflamed. Some skin complaints (dealt with later on in this chapter), affect the feet also, or it may be a dietary deficiency such as a lack of fresh food. Increase your pets supply of greenstuffs and as an added measure obtain some soluble vitamin drops available from pet shops and add the recommended dosage to the water bottle. Bathing the soles of the feet with a dilute antiseptic or smearing on some herbal skin balm will aid recovery.

Injuries

Occasionally guinea-pigs may injure their front or rear legs by getting claws caught in wire mesh and wrenching themselves out, or falling awkwardly. They will limp and may spend time just resting. If you are assured that the limb is not broken or the guinea-pig is not in pain, then allow your pet to rest until recovered. Usually recovery takes about a week. A claw may similarly be lost and provided there is no sign of infection, simply apply antiseptic until the new claw grows through.

Mouth and Teeth

Guinea-pigs have four front incisor teeth and four sets of molar or cheek teeth. These latter teeth are situated far back in the jaw and a lot of owners are unaware that they exist. In between the front and rear teeth is a gap called the Diastema, used for sucking in the cheeks and so avoiding the accidental swallowing of unpalatable gnawing materials. Take a close look at your pets teeth. The front incisors should meet together with the top ones slightly overlying the bottom ones.

Usually feeding a correct diet including plenty of hard grinding matter will avoid any dental problems but there are a few that do occur from time to time.

Teeth Loss

A common problem is the loss of the incisor teeth usually through your pet leaping prematurely from your arms onto the ground. As they tend to land nose first this results in some or all of their incisor teeth being knocked out. If only the upper incisors have been lost it may be necessary to trim the lower ones down to allow for even re-growth of both sets of teeth. The guinea-pig may experience difficulty in picking up harder foodstuffs so it is a good idea to grate things like carrot, and finely shred greens.

If, after teeth loss, your pet seems to be having difficulty eating dry food and is losing weight, you will have to syringe feed him until the new teeth have grown.

As a guinea-pigs teeth grow at a phenomenal rate, something like 1mm per day, after about 3 days the guinea-pig should be able to feed himself again.

I syringe feed my sick guinea-pigs with is a mixture of brown or wholemeal bread or instant mashed potato, cucumber, a little milk (or fortified drink mix and water), and several pet vitamin drops all whizzed around in a blender until a smooth fairly runny paste has formed. This mixture will only keep for a short time so a fresh amount will need to be made each day. Rough quantities are 1 slice of bread to several slices of cucumber. Alternative fresh foods such as carrot or banana can be used. If you use banana, don't be alarmed if your mixture goes black! It is just the banana discolouring, the taste will still be fine.

The syringe will need the narrow tip cut off so that you can suck the mixture up into the tube. Towel wrap your guinea-pig and putting the syringe sideways into his mouth feed him as much as he will take in one sitting. Repeat every three hours during the day until he is eating by himself.

Overgrown Teeth

Sometimes all the incisor teeth become excessively overgrown, usually a dietary problem but occasionally the result of a misaligned jaw. The guinea-pig will not be able to close its mouth properly and the teeth may be curved inwards.

The teeth will need to be filed down or broken off at the

correct place so that they re-align properly. He may then suffer no further problems but in some instances he will need them filed on a regular basis. You should get this done initially by an expert but if you feel confident it is something that can be done at home using recommended equipment.

The molar teeth are more of a problem if they become overgrown. Because they are so far back it is difficult to see them unless special equipment is used to hold the mouth open. The outward signs are that the guinea-pig will leave pieces of uneaten food lying in the bowl or on the floor of the cage. He may start to dribble and lose weight as more food is left untouched.

Overgrown molars curve over the tongue in spur-like projections and may cut into the tongue causing the guinea-pig distress. They should be filed back down until flat and level. It is preferable to get this done by an expert as it is a more tricky procedure requiring specialist equipment.

Mouth Sores

Some guinea-pigs can develop mouth sores as a result of eating too many acidic foods such as apple and tomato, or a fungal infection. If he develops crusty looking sores at the corners of his mouth or on his upper lip, discontinue feeding acidic fruits immediately. If the condition remains or worsens, the guinea-pig will need a course of prescription only medication to clear them up.

Diarrhoea.

If a guinea-pig has over-indulged on greenstuffs or eaten frosted greens, the result may be diarrhoea or scours. Guinea-pigs normally have two types of droppings. The ones scattered about the cage floor are dry, brown, sausage-shaped pellets. The other sort are softer pellets usually taken straight from the anus and re-ingested. This is called Coprophragy and is quite normal; similar to chewing the cud in cattle. The soft droppings are full of nutrients, enzymes and bacteria vital to the guinea-pigs health.

Diarrhoea results in the normal dry droppings becoming liquid. Stop feeding all greenstuffs for 2 or 3 days, restricting your pet to dry food and hay only. Shepherds Purse, the whole plant, or a small bramble or raspberry leaf with the thorns removed, fed daily may aid recovery as these plants have astringent qualities, helping to dry up diarrhoea.

If the diarrhoea is prolonged, becomes foul-smelling or mucous is present then it may be a more serious problem. Listlessness or irregular breathing in addition to the diarrhoea may indicate liver or kidney trouble and expert help from a Veterinary Surgeon should be sought as soon as possible.

Poisoning

This is quite a common Summer problem when gardeners have been using sprays and deterrents in the garden and farmers have been spraying their crops. Guinea-pigs are usually put out on the lawn for the first time as the weather improves and this is when they are prone to ingesting or inhaling poisons.

Another way guinea-pigs become poisoned is by eating a poisonous plant along with grass. Young pigs in particular may not be as selective in what they eat so it is most important that outdoor runs are placed on grass which does not contain any of the plants mentioned in the Chapter on Feeding.

A poisoned guinea-pig will become ill very quickly. He may tremble violently and twitch. His eyes may roll and his breathing will be very rapid or irregular. His body may go rigid and then floppy and feel cold especially the ears. He will be unable to co-ordinate movement and be in a state of collapse. An ingested poison may give him diarrhoea. Urgent action is required in order to save his life.

Guinea-pigs cannot vomit. Any toxin which enters their body has to be flushed through as rapidly as possible to be voided along with urine and faeces. Re-hydration fluids available from Veterinary Surgeries must be syringed into the ill guinea-pig as quickly as possible in small but regular doses. Sometimes if it is known what poison was ingested, an antidote can be given. In any event of poisoning, time is of the essence and help should be sought immediately.

Heatstroke

In summer months another problem for guinea-pigs is heatstroke. A guinea-pig suffering from heatstroke will feel very hot, damp and limp. He will be breathing rapidly and have a running nose and be dribbling. His discomfort will be very obvious.

To cool your guinea-pig down, soak a towel in cold water and wrap him up in it. NEVER, NEVER submerge a guinea-pig with heatstroke into a bucket of cold water. The shock could kill him. Keep replacing the wet towels with freshly wetted ones until the guinea-pig shows signs of recovery. Make sure he has a drink available, preferably re-hydration fluid to replace lost body salts.

Once the guinea-pig recovers he must be kept indoors until completely dry, overnight if necessary.

Obviously the situation of the hutch and run is of paramount importance as discussed under Housing. Sometimes however even the best situated hutch can become hot. Some ways in which you can avoid heatstroke are to hang wet towels over the front of the hutch or over the outdoor run. These will provide shade as well as lowering the temperature. Have an electric fan inside a shed, outhouse or garage. Put up blinds or curtains to keep out the sun. Always ensure your pet has plenty of fresh cool drinking water.

Eyes

E ye problems can occur if straw is used or the hay is particularly sharp or thistley. Pieces can poke the eyelid or the eye itself causing inflammation and weeping. The eyeball becomes opaque if damaged, sometimes the whole surface turning milky white. This will last several days before clearing.

Foreign Bodies

Check the eye to ensure that nothing is lodged in the soft tissue surrounding the eyeball. If there is a seed husk or other foreign body caught in the lid, remove carefully using tweezers or the folded edge of a soft handkerchief. Then bathe the eye in saline solution until better. If the eye continues to be inflamed and watery, take your pet along to an expert as prescription only eye-drops or cream may be needed.

Fatty Eye

Sometimes guinea-pigs develop a condition called fatty eye. The lower eyelid appears to droop and the inside tissue bulges out slightly. Although unsightly this is usually an old age problem and nothing to worry about.

Blindness

Cataracts and blindness do occur in guinea-pigs of all ages. Some breeders believe that certain varieties are more predisposed to cataracts than others. A guinea-pig may be born with cataracts or develop them in one or both eyes at any age. The eye is opaque and the animal sightless or partially sighted. A blind guinea-pig can however do very well without its sight and so there is no need to think of having it put to sleep simply because it can no longer see. Providing it is kept in familiar surroundings the other senses of hearing and smell will compensate for the lack of sight.

Do not however breed from a guinea-pig with any eyesight problem as you may be perpetuating the weakness along further generations. (See pictures on page 54).

Ears

Ears sometimes become torn during a fight or a mother will occasionally chew her newborn babies ear whilst removing it from its birth membrane. These injuries will heal up on their own although if a large chunk has been bitten out you can bathe the ear in antiseptic to prevent infection.

Ear Mites

Internally, there may be a build up of wax and dirt which can be regularly removed with a moistened cotton bud. Sometimes excessive black, waxy-looking debris accompanied by much ear scratching may mean the presence of mites and these can be removed with eardrops. Those suitable for ear mites in cats and dogs are very effective. Clean thoroughly inside both ears with a moistened cotton bud to remove the dirt then apply 2

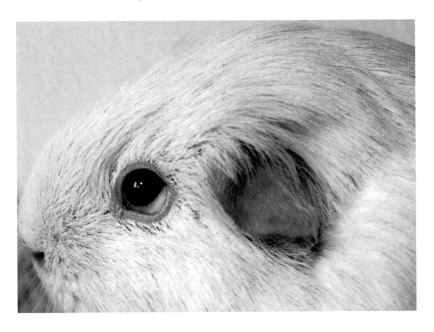

A Guinea-pig with fatty eye

Cataracts in an Abyssinian Guinea-pig.

drops into each ear. Repeat for four or five days.

Colds.

If you hear your guinea-pig sneezing a lot and he has a runny nose and eyes, he may have a chill. Listen to his breathing. If it is noisy or rattling, bring him indoors and put him in a cardboard box lined with paper and hay and keep in a warm room with plenty of food and fresh vegetables until better. A smear of Herbal vapour-rub around the top inside edge of the box will ease his breathing.

Better still, place the cardboard box inside a larger box with a gap at one end big enough to place a hot water bottle. The bottle will be wedged against the outer wall of the smaller box and the inner wall of the larger box. The guinea-pig can then nestle up to the warm wall of the cardboard box but is also able to move away from the heat if necessary. He can then be kept warm during the night when the central heating may be turned off.

Skin and Hair Problems

Hormonal Hair Loss

Sometimes sows who have had litters suffer from hair loss particularly along the back bone and sometimes underneath. This hair loss is quite common and may be due to the strain upon the body's resources during pregnancy and milk production and/or hormonal fluctuations. It will grow back in time but a vitamin supplement may be of benefit which can be added to the drinking water. You can buy these from pet shops.

As a matter of course I always give pregnant and lactating sows a daily bowl of brown bread and fortified drink mix. This is greedily gobbled up by the mum and is often eaten by the young guinea-pigs as well. Extra dry foods and greens are also given at this time along with plenty of fresh hay.

Parasitic Problems

Lice

An external form of parasitic infestation, commonly called running lice, may occasionally be found on guinea-pigs. Check your animals coat for the presence of small creamy white wriggly objects close to the base of the hair follicles.

Sometimes what are called "Static Lice" will be seen. These are stuck on the hair shaft and look like brownish grey specks of dirt. The usual place to see them is around the hindquarters or in advanced cases, up around the neck and chin region also.

They are extremely difficult to dislodge and will remain on the hair shaft even after shampooing. The only way to remove them is by using a special nit comb, but unless you wish to show your guinea-pig, this is a somewhat laborious task. Unless found in considerable numbers, lice and static lice do not affect the guinea-pigs health as adversely as other skin complaints. However it is better to deal with the problem than leave it unattended.

To eradicate both you need to use an anti-parasitic shampoo or spray used for eradicating lice and mites in small animals and birds. There are several types available from Pet Shops or your Vet. Use according to the instructions. Please note that these lice cannot live on humans.

Mange

Mange is a mite infestation to which guinea-pigs may be prone and is often first noticed when the animal appears to be balding.

If your pet seems to be scratching more than usual, and has thinning hair or bald patches, particularly round the head and shoulders, or underneath and on the insides of the legs, this may be due to Mange. Often the skin is much redder than normal, and sometimes broken where the guinea-pig has scratched himself. Seen in the light the coat looks dusty with no lustre and may contain lots of black specks of dirt. It has a spikey or "staring" appearance.

If mange is left untreated the guinea-pig's health will be affected by the constant irritation of the mites. He will become very thin and miserable. In severe cases guinea-pigs can become completely bald with deep bleeding lesions.

Fortunately mange can be effectively treated with a prescription only anti-parasitic drug obtainable from your Vet which is given by injection. When combined with regular shampooing at home with an anti-parasitic shampoo this is an effective deterrent against mange.

When using an anti-parasitic shampoo it is important to ensure that the shampoo covers the whole animal, including inside the ears but avoid the mouth and eye area.

Parasitic complaints found on guinea-pigs cannot be transferred to humans so you can still handle your guinea-pig if he has mange.

Fungal complaints

If your guinea-pig is suffering from a Fungal complaint the skin will look dry and scaly and the coat greasy. If the centre of the back, often the worse affected place, is rubbed with a finger the hair will easily come away in clumps. The hair follicles will have what looks like thick dandruff attached to them at the roots. The guinea-pigs feet may look red and blistered as well. He may react violently to being touched as his skin will be more sensitive than usual.

There is more than one fungal infection to which guinea-pigs may be prone. A few of these complaints can be transferred to humans so always wash your hands thoroughly after handling a pig with suspected fungal infection.

To deal with fungal infection you need to buy a medicated shampoo for Seborrhoeic Dermatitis and dandruff and wash the guinea-pig weekly until the condition clears.

If the fungal infection is severe or systemic the guinea-pig will need a course of anti-fungal dipping solution or oral drugs.

Sometimes a guinea-pig may suffer from a combined Fungal and Parasitic infection. In this case you will need to follow a programme of treatment which is effective for both complaints and includes prescription only medications combined with shampoos.

In all cases of skin disease and infection, thoroughly clean and disinfect the guinea-pigs cage and eating and drinking utensils before returning the animal to it. Use an anti-bacterial and anti-fungal disinfectant for maximum protection against re-infection.

Impaction in Boars.

Older boars occasionally suffer from Impaction, caused by the softer pellets, the ones they re-ingest, being unable to be passed through the anal opening situated immediately behind the penis. Normal pellets can still be expelled but the soft ones form a large lump which is clearly visible when the boar is picked up.

The only treatment for this condition is to expel the lumped together pellets manually as soon as they build up. It is not particularly pleasant for the guinea-pig or the owner but unfortunately essential to maintain his good health.

Gently squeeze the lump out of the anus, a smear of lubricating ointment may help the process, and that is all that needs to be done until the next time. The guinea-pig will probably squeal loudly as you are doing this but if you are gentle he should not suffer.

Sawdust Impaction

Boars can also become impacted if they are bedded on sawdust. Boars scent their cages by smearing a creamy secretion from the anus. The secretion is foul smelling to a human nose, something between over boiled cabbage and old socks!, but presumably delightful to a sow. The boar will go around its cage lowering his bottom and dragging it across the floor scenting it.

If the cage floor is covered in sawdust this will be drawn up inside the anal sac causing a blockage and possible infection. This is why I strongly recommend only hay as a floor covering.

The penis can also be affected in a similar way. Sawdust and debris may attach itself to the penis which the boar will not then be able to retract. The whole area may become swollen and infected.

If this happens the boars penis and anal area need to be washed with a mild soap, preferably an anti-bacterial liquid soap and dried carefully. This may be all that is necessary but if the area continues to look swollen and inflamed an antiseptic cream will need to be applied until the infection has gone.

The cream is a prescription only medication so you will need to visit an expert.

Urine Infections.

Urine infections are a relatively common complaint. Both boars and sows can be affected, although, as in humans, it is more often the females who suffer from these problems. Personal experience seems also to indicate that it is the long-haired more than short-haired guinea-pigs who get urine complaints.

This may be because the urine soaks into the long hair around her rear end and this constant dampness is an ideal breeding ground for germs.

Signs of Urine Infection and Treatment

The signs to look for are a constantly wet bottom, but also a strong, unpleasant smell around the anus and possibly some crusting of urine on the anus. In more severe cases the surrounding skin may become burned by the urine. It will be red and sore with some hair loss. Both boars and sows, suffering from a urine infection, may squeak with pain on passing urine.

The most effective cure is a prescription only antibiotic. A weeks course should be sufficient to clear up the problem. Meticulous hygiene must be maintained and regular bathing and hair trimming if the affected animal is long haired.

Flystrike

Meticulous hygiene is especially important during summer months because if the guinea-pig is left with a wet, smelly bottom it becomes an attractive breeding ground for flies.

Flystrike occurs when flies lay eggs on the animal and the hatched out maggots then eat their way into the flesh, nearly always with fatal results.

Regular bathing of the guinea-pigs rear and thorough drying followed by a dusting of antiseptic talcum powder (available from pet shops) should prevent Flystrike.

Reproduction.

One of the greatest joys of keeping guinea-pigs is watching them through all stages of life including pregnancy, birth and the rearing of their young. Obviously careful thought and planning has to be given beforehand as to whether you have adequate housing for the increased numbers and can afford to feed and look after them. Also, whether the young are to be kept. If not, then suitable homes need to be found. It would be unthinkable to condemn your pets offspring to a miserable existence with an unsuitable owner simply as a result of your desire for your guinea-pig to have babies.

Bear in mind that you may have 4 or more young and they can become sexually mature at 4 weeks old. Young boars will need separating from their mother and from their sisters at this age. The best age to mate your sows for the first time is between 4 and 9 months old. She will then give birth before she is one year old. Sows can become pregnant as young as 5-6 weeks old but a pregnancy at this age is not recommended. Her body is too small and immature and miscarriage is an increased risk. Sows mated for the first time when over one year old can be more prone to Toxaemia and birth difficulties. Boars are best mated at a young age and can be placed with a sow from six weeks old.

Length of Gestation

Sows give birth to their young after a very long pregnancy lasting approximately 70 days. Compared to a rabbits pregnancy of around 30 days this is indeed a long time but the end result is worth the wait. Baby guinea-pigs are adorable, exact replicas of their parents from the minute they are born, fully furred and with their eyes open. There are very few animals that are born at such an advanced stage of development, able to move speedily about and nibble at solid food from a day old.

Sows come into season approximately once every 3 weeks so to ensure a successful conception it is usually necessary to leave the boar and sow together for a month or more. I tend to leave them together until the pregnancy is confirmed by feeling movements of the unborn young. By this stage the pregnancy is at least 6 weeks advanced.

Do not leave the boar with the sow after she has had her babies. He may mate with her again immediately after the birth which would not be good for her health or that of her suckling offspring. His attentions to the female may also result in babies being trampled and injured.

Pregnancy Record Cards

It is a good idea to keep a pregnancy record card. I keep separate breeding cards for my stock which on one side gives details of the boar and the sow, their age and variety, date of pairing, date of removal of the boar, date of birth, number of young and sex. On the other side of the card I keep a more detailed diary of events including when movements were first felt, weight of sow throughout pregnancy, health problems, date of separation of pelvic bones (a precursor to birth), condition of young, condition of sow after birth, and any other information up to weaning of the young.

Pregnancy Pointers

Usually the first sign that your sow is pregnant will be her increased thirst. This occurs in about the third week of pregnancy. She may also be more aggressive than usual towards the boar and other sows. Gradually her sides begin to feel more rounded and firmer than usual and her weight will increase. In the sixth to seventh week of pregnancy movements can be felt of the unborn young. Her appetite will increase around this time and extra greens and dry mix should be provided.

During the last couple of weeks before birth the sows girth will increase considerably. The movements of the young can be pretty powerful at this time although they never seem to bother the sow. Some sows may become quite bow-legged and cumbersome in their movements although they are still able to move speedily if necessary.

At this stage I provide all my sows with a bowl of brown bread and original flavour fortified drink mix. Most eat this readily although it may take a couple of days for them to take to it.

As birth approaches the pelvic bones will be easily felt just above the anal opening. These two small pointed bones will move apart to allow for the birth of the young. Sometimes this process may take several days or only 24 hours.

"Pixie" a few days before birth.

Sybil with her week old litter.

Movements of the young will decrease at this time because they are so tightly packed inside the sow, although they should still be felt. It is possible by putting your ear close to the sows flanks to hear the young grinding their teeth!

Birth

When birth is imminent the pelvic bones will move apart to about a thumbs width. The sow may scrape away an area of bedding in her cage to form a shallow nest in which she will have her young. They are born head first and the sow aids their birth by bending down and pulling the babies out with her teeth.

Each baby guinea-pig has its own foetal sac, umbilical cord and placenta. As the baby is born the sow cleans it thoroughly, cutting through the membrane at the head end and thoroughly washing this area to remove any mucous in the mouth or nose. This enables the baby guinea-pig to take its first breath. The umbilical cord is snipped off with the teeth and the placenta eaten, although if her litter is a large one then one or two placentas may be left. The entire baby is washed vigorously until it is clean and almost dry.

Most sows give birth to their babies in fairly quick succession, so a litter of say four babies will arrive within the space of about half an hour to an hour. Often the sow will give birth to her young in the early hours of the morning but birth can occur at any time of the day or night.

Sybil in her last stages of pregnancy.

Four 6 week old babies

Usually no remains of afterbirth can be seen and there is very little blood. The babies will crowd around their mother all beautifully clean and fluffy, eyes open and fully alert, looking as though they have been there forever and not just a few minutes.

The average weight of newborn guinea-pigs is 3oz although 2oz or as much as 5oz is not uncommon. A normal litter size is 2 to 4 young although some sows may just have 1 baby and others as many as 6.

Feeding and Weaning

Sows have only two nipples, so if the litter is a large one then the babies have to patiently wait their turn to feed. I continue to provide a bowl of brown bread and fortified drink mix for up to two weeks after birth and this is taken readily often by the babies as well as mum. Extra dry mix and greens should also be given to help the sow produce enough milk. She may drink more water than usual so ensure she has a fresh supply daily.

The baby guinea-pigs should be weaned at four weeks old. At this stage I separate the boars, but leave one or more sows with mum. They may continue to feed from her for another couple of weeks until the sows milk dries up. This prevents any possibility of her nipples becoming engorged with milk and a very painful inflammation called Mastitis resulting.

Pregnancy Complications

With most sows there are no pregnancy complications and the whole process is a joy to watch but occasionally things do go wrong and so you need be especially observant at this time.

Miscarriage

Sometimes a sow may miscarry four to five weeks into her pregnancy. There will be slight blood loss for 3-4 days. The blood will be bright red and slightly thicker than normal and may be crusted around her anus. Although the sow will not be ill, she may be quieter than normal for a few days. Do not try to re-mate her for at least one month after a miscarriage.

Toxaemia

In the last stage of pregnancy, if the sow is sitting huddled not eating and appears listless, this is a warning that she may have pregnancy toxaemia. Movements of the unborn young may decrease or become feeble. As the condition worsens, the sow will start slobbering and her eyes appear dull or sunken. This is very serious indeed. Toxaemia in guinea-pigs can strike for no known reason and is very often fatal.

If your guinea-pig develops any of the early symptoms of toxaemia during pregnancy, bring her indoors straight away to keep her warm and quiet. However, excessive heat can worsen the condition so, if it is high summer, keep her somewhere cool and undisturbed instead.

Give her a Calcium and Vitamin D supplement, available from chemist shops. The "berries" are easy to administer and contain both calcium and Vitamin D in the one capsule. Snip the coating of the berry and squeeze the contents into the guinea-pigs mouth. Repeat each morning and evening.

Provide her also with a bowl of brown bread and fortified drink mix as this is a good source of vitamins and minerals. If she will not eat it from the bowl syringe feed her if you can get hold of some syringes or else use a coffee spoon or teaspoon.

Provide the ill sow with plenty of fresh leafy green vegetables or grass if it is summer, to encourage her appetite. If her condition worsens she will have to go to an expert for more drastic treatment. Options are to give the sow an injection of Oxytocin to bring about labour and birth, or perform a Caesarean. Both these procedures are risky and are very much dependent on how ill the sow is.

Toxaemia may also occur after the sow has given birth. The symptoms are the same. The sow may nudge her babies away, not letting them suckle and will sit hunched, listless and possibly dribbling. Immediate action must be taken to avoid losing both mother and babies. Follow the same procedure as for pregnancy toxaemia. It may be necessary to foster or handfeed the babies whilst the sow recovers.

Dead Babies

Sometimes sows will have a litter in which some or all of the babies are dead. There may be several reasons for this. The first baby to be born may be very large and the birth process long and painful. The sow is exhausted and traumatised by this and has to rest and recover. Subsequent babies may be born without any difficulty or not, depending on how quickly the sow recovers.

The sow may give birth to her babies so quickly that she cannot cope with the all important cleaning process for each one. If two are born in quick succession the first baby will be left while the sow concentrates her efforts on the new arrival. A baby may be born still encased in its foetal sac and will suffocate if left.

A sow may give birth prematurely. The babies will be very small only 1-1.5oz in weight. The hair will be very short and the claws white and soft. These babies will not survive unfortunately even if they are alive initially. They are unable to suckle and if handfed will only live a few days.

Resuscitation

If you are present at or immediately after a sow has given birth and you discover a baby lying motionless on the floor of the cage, which the sow has been unable to attend to, you may be able to intervene to save its life. There is a great risk of failure however so do not be distressed if you are unsuccessful. If the foetal sac is still covering the baby tear it away from the head end

72

and expel any mucous by cupping the baby securely in both hands holding it above your head and doing a sharp downward movement. This may sound drastic but it is effective. Next rub the baby with both hands or with a piece of soft towel removing any remaining foetal sac and warming and invigorating its body. The baby should cough and start breathing on its own.

If you are lucky enough to succeed and the baby starts breathing you must keep it warm either by tucking it against your own body or using a hot water bottle and blankets. When the baby is fully alert and standing, it can be returned to the mother. Rub it with her scent so she will accept it as one of her own. Do not give the baby anything to eat or drink unless after 24 hours the sow has still not accepted it.

Fostering and Hand Rearing

Fostering

If the sow dies or is not in a fit state to care for her baby or babies, you can try to foster them. Fostering can work if you have a sow with a newly born litter who will accept the orphan babies as her own. Rub the orphans with the smell of the foster mum and that of her own offspring and gradually introduce them to her. If she accepts them you must provide her with extra sustenance in the form of brown bread and fortified drink mix to enable her to cope with the suddenly enlarged family. Extra fresh food and dry mix should also be provided.

Hand-rearing

If the sow will not accept the orphan babies as her own you can try to hand-rear them. However success is not guaranteed so do not be heartbroken if they do not survive. Warmth is the first priority. Put the babies into a small box lined with paper and soft hay and place a hot water bottle, wrapped in a towel or similar covering, at one end. Place the babies next to the hot water bottle. They will be able to regulate their own body temperature by moving nearer or further away from the bottle as necessary. Do not feed the babies for the first day. If they were being suckled by their mother, her milk would not flow immediately after birth so it is important that you treat them the same.

Feeding Baby Guinea-pigs

When it is time to feed them make up a small amount of warm fortified milk drink and soak some brown bread into it. Pick up the first baby and hold it securely. Using a small teaspoon put a small amount of the mixture up to the baby guinea-pigs mouth and let it sip. Do not tip it down the baby's throat as it will go into its lungs and kill it. This is a time-consuming process and the baby will not take more than a teaspoon of mixture at any one time. Every 2-3 hours and during the night the babies will need feeding for the first week.

After feeding the baby must be stimulated to defecate. If you watch a normal situation of mother and babies you will observe the babies raising their bottoms towards their mum.

74

"Sybil" and her babies.
Guinea-pigs may have from 1 - 6 young in a litter.

Pixie with her four babies.

She then licks them vigorously so stimulating them to pass urine and pellets. To emulate this action yourself, dip one end of a cotton bud into warm water and pass it over the baby pigs anus several times until it passes a pellet. You may not be successful every time but you must repeat this procedure after every feed until they are able to pass pellets and urine by themselves.

As young baby guinea-pigs will nibble at solids from a day old provide a small amount of dry mix and various pieces of fresh fruit and vegetable to encourage them to feed themselves. You can also place a small bowl of their brown bread and fortified milk drink in the box, but do not stop handfeeding them until you are sure they are eating a good amount of the mixture themselves and eating their dry mix and fresh foods also.

From my observations of newborn guinea-pigs they seem to know instinctively how to wash themselves and will nibble experimentally at hard foodstuffs very soon after birth. However it may be a good idea to place in with the babies a newly weaned youngster if you can obtain one, to help teach your babies how to feed themselves. Even an older sow, as long as she is gentle and placid will be acceptable. Watch them very carefully to make sure the older one is not bullying the younger ones.

Conclusion

The aim of this book has been to provide the sort of detailed information on how to look after your pet guinea-pig knowledgeably and successfully. It provides detailed advice on where to go and how to choose your first guinea-pig through to daily maintenance, detecting common problems and breeding and rearing young.

As stated at the beginning of this book, guinea-pigs are hardly the dull, stolid animals people have been led to believe. They are intelligent, funny and fascinating to watch. The amazing sight of guinea-pig babies less than 24 hours old running around their cage nibbling at bits of hay, or the elaborate gestures and vocal sounds of a group of pigs squabbling over a plate of fresh vegetables, or an ill guinea-pig suddenly perking up and eating its first mouthful of fresh grass; all these elements must surely make them one of the most rewarding pets around.

If you feel inspired to further your knowledge and gain a professional qualification in Rodentology, the Cambridge Cavy Trust and Guinea-Pig Hospital, as well as nursing sick animals and re-homing others, run a Diploma course.

This is a Distance Learning Training Scheme lasting eighteen months or three years depending upon the student's work and home commitments.

It covers the Physiology and Anatomy of small rodents, Diseases and Medication and includes Workshops and the chance of hands-on experience of working with guinea-pigs, chinchillas, gerbils, hamsters and other pet rodents.

If you would like details of this course and some general information on the Trust and how to join the address is given below :

C.C.T Veterinary Hospital
Top Farm Bungalow
Alconbury, Huntingdon
Cambridgeshire
PE17 5EW

Tel: 01480 455346

The main bulk of the Trust's work is still nursing and re-homing abandoned, ill and maltreated guinea-pigs and other pets, and volunteers are always welcomed to help in any capacity.

Index

Index

Index

Index

Index

Index